WELCOME TO
KIRSTEN'S WORLD ♥ 1854
Growing Up in Pioneer America

THE AMERICAN GIRLS COLLECTION®

Published by Pleasant Company Publications
© Copyright 1999 by Pleasant Company
All rights reserved. No part of this book may be used or reproduced
in any manner whatsoever without written permission except in the
case of brief quotations embodied in critical articles and reviews.
For information, address: Book Editor,
Pleasant Company Publications,
8400 Fairway Place, P.O. Box 620998,
Middleton, WI 53562.

Printed in Singapore.
99 00 01 02 03 04 05 TWP 10 9 8 7 6 5 4 3 2 1
The American Girls Collection®, Kirsten®, and Kirsten Larson®
are trademarks of Pleasant Company.

Written by Susan Sinnott
Edited by Jodi Evert, Michelle Jones, and Yvette LaPierre
Historical and Editorial Consulting by American Historical Publications
Designed and Art Directed by Mengwan Lin, Ingrid Slamer, and Jane S.Varda
Produced by Mary Cudnohfsky and Cheryll Mellenthin
Cover Illustration by Reneé Graef
Interior Illustrations by Chris Duke, Chris Gargan, David Henderson,
Laszlo Kubinyi, and Susan McAliley
Researched by Nina Clark, Mary Davison, Sally Jacobs, and Sally Wood
Prop Research and Styling by Jean doPico
Photography by Connie Russell and Jamie Young

Special thanks to the Minnesota Historical Society

Library of Congress Cataloging-in-Publication Data
Sinnott, Susan.
Welcome to Kirsten's world, 1854 / [written by Susan Sinnott].
p. cm. — (The American girls collection)
Summary: Presents a look at daily life in pioneer America during the 1850s by following
a family that emigrates from Sweden to Minnesota.
ISBN 1-56247-770-6
1. West (U.S.)—Social life and customs—19th century—Juvenile literature. 2. West (U.S.)—History—1848-
1860—Juvenile literature. 3. Frontier and pioneer life—West (U.S.)—Juvenile literature. 4. Pioneer children—
West (U.S.)—Social life and customs—Juvenile literature. 5. Swedish Americans—West (U.S.)—Social life and
customs—Juvenile literature.
[1. West (U.S.)—Social life and customs. 2. Frontier and pioneer life—West (U.S.) 3. Swedish Americans.]
I. Title. II. Series.
F593.S55 1999 978'.02—dc21 98-54738 CIP AC

Introduction: Pages 2-3—America chest, Nordiska Museet, Stockholm; trunk and belongings, Erlander Home Museum, Rockford, IL; girls leaving, Vesterheim Norwegian-American Museum from the exhibit With Our Hands and Minds; kitten basket and toy horse, Erlander Home Museum, Rockford, IL; Dala Painting, American Swedish Institute; Kirsten and Mama, illustration by Renée Graef from *Meet Kirsten*; Pages 4-5—sailing for America, *The Emigrants* by Knut Ekwall, in the collection of the American Scandinavian Foundation, courtesy of Lena Biörck Kaplan; the frontier, *The Emigrant Train, Colorado* by Samuel Coleman, St. Johnsbury Athenaeum; *Uncle Tom's Cabin*, Charles L. Blockson Afro-American Collection, Temple University;

Chapter One: Pages 6-7—Castle Garden, New-York Historical Society; captain and ship, Mystic Seaport Museum, Inc.; Pages 8-9—Swede Town, residences in Swede Town about 1880, Chicago Historical Society, ICHi-01417; *Hemlandet*, Newspaper Collections, Library of the State Historical Society of Wisconsin; letters, Bishop Hill Archives; business is booming, Chicago Historical Society, ICHi-17661; streets of Chicago, Chicago Historical Society, ICHi-03799; cobblestone streets, engraving from *Ballou's Pictorial Drawing Room Companion*, Oct. 15, 1859, Boston, MA, Chicago Historical Society, ICHi-01955;

Chapter Two: Pages 12-13—axe, State Historical Society of Wisconsin; saw, Barbara Johnson Antiques, Rockford, IL; log cabin, State Historical Society of Wisconsin's Old World Wisconsin Outdoor Museum; Pages 14-15—soddie, Nebraska State Historical Society; prairie schooner, National Archives (NWDNS-69-N-13606C); frame house, State Historical Society of Wisconsin, WHi (D32)810; Indian summer home, *Permanent Residence, Sioux* by Seth Eastman, Minnesota Historical Society; leather thong tepee ornament, Buffalo Bill Historical Center, Cody, WY, gift of Anne Black; buffalo hooves tepee ornament, courtesy of the Ethnology Program, Provincial Museum of Alberta, Edmonton (H89.220.72); tepees, *Sioux Camp* by Karl Bodmer, JAM.1986.49.375, Joslyn Art Museum, Omaha, NE; wigwam, The Field Museum, CSA 14494 Birchbark Lodge; Pages 16-17—barn raising, State Historical Society of Wisconsin, WHi(X3)40239; quilt, Helen Louise Allen Textile Collection, University of Wisconsin–Madison; *Cornhusking at Nantucket*, 07.68, by Eastman Johnson, The Metropolitan Museum of Art; quilting bee, State Historical Society of North Dakota; piano accordion, Erlander Home Museum, Rockford, IL; scutching bee, Linton Park, *Flax Scutching Bee*, gift of Edgar William and Bernice Chrysler Garabisch, © 1998 Board of Trustees, National Gallery of Art, Washington, DC; Pages 18-19—country dance, courtesy of Crabtree Publishing Company; valentine writer, courtesy of Phillips International Fine Art Auctioneers; scutching knife, distaff, mangling board, and betrothal chest, Nordiska Museet; gloves, Dorling Kindersley Ltd.; hymnal, Erlander Home Museum, Rockford, IL; courting blanket, American Museum of National History; courting flute, catalogue no. 200588, Department of Anthropology, Smithsonian Institution, photo courtesy Glenbow (P 3205-625); engagement picture, Minnesota Historical Society; Pages 20-21—minister's chest, Nordic Heritage Museum, Seattle, WA; wedding party and wedding couple, from the Collections of the American Swedish Institute; suitors' spoons, Erlander Home Museum, Rockford, IL; wedding gown, University of Wisconsin, Steven's Point Costume Collection; wedding basket, Barbara Johnson Antiques, Rockford, IL; bridal crown, Erlander Home Museum, Rockford, IL; wedding bells, Erlander Home Museum, Rockford, IL; hanging crown, Swedish-American Museum, Chicago, IL, photo by Connie Russell, Orchid Photographics; candelabra, Erlander Home Museum, Rockford, IL;

Chapter Three: Pages 22-23—flax, Corbis/Jacqui Hurst; daylilies, Corbis/Hal Horwitz; hay rake, Barbara Johnson Antiques, Rockford, IL; Pages 24-25—hide scraper, Minnesota Historical Society; Pages 30-31—doctor on horseback, photo courtesy of Siskiyou County Museum, Yreka, CA; stethoscope, State Historical Society of Wisconsin; doctor and patient, *The Doctor* by Arthur Miles, The Maas Gallery, London, UK/Bridgeman Art Library, London/New York (MAA55004); doctor's saw, Minnesota Historical Society; medicine wagon and receipt book, Minnesota Historical Society; medicine bottles, private collection of Jane Geving, Middleton Antiques Mall; medicine chest, Oregon Historical Society, 2733; illness and epidemics, Nebraska State Historical Society; Pages 32-33—rag dolls, courtesy of The Strong Museum, Rochester, NY © 1875; children's chores, National Archives (NWDNS-115-JAD-224); paper dolls, Minnesota Historical Society; school, Property of the Division of Special Collections & University Archives, University of Oregon Library System; ice skates, Barbara Johnson Antiques, Rockford, IL; top, Minnesota Historical Society; school books, Oregon Historical Society; outdoor games, *Snap the Whip* by Winslow Homer, The Metropolitan Museum of Art, gift of Christian A. Zabriskie, 1950 (50.41) photograph © 1992 The Metropolitan Museum of Art; sled, Barbara Johnson Antiques, Rockford, IL; Pages 34-35—turtle charms, detail from photograph, courtesy Department of Library Services, American Museum of Natural History; cradleboard, San Diego Museum of Man; "third mother," National Museum of American Art, Washington, DC/Art Resource; tan doll, Colter Bay Indian Art Museum; red doll, San Diego Museum of Man; tiny tepees and household skills, National Museum of Natural History, Smithsonian Institution; Sioux Baby Moccasins, Glenbow Collection,

Calgary, Alberta, Canada (AF 3548 A-B); games, by De Cost Smith, from the book *Growing Up in America: 1830-1860* by Evelyn Toynton; lacrosse stick and ball, and ring and pin game, Minnesota Historical Society; toy canoe, Colter Bay Indian Art Museum; Pages 36-37—hoop, State Historical Society of Wisconsin (1956.1947a); Sunday best, Historic Northampton, Northampton, MA; calico dress, State Historical Society of Wisconsin; pantalettes, State Historical Society of Wisconsin (1967.397.20); girl, courtesy George Eastman House; sunbonnet, State Historical Society of Wisconsin; purse, Barbara Johnson Antiques, Rockford, IL; fashionable dresses, Oshkosh Public Museum; chatelaine, stockings and boots, corset and chemise, hair jewelry, and petticoat, State Historical Society of Wisconsin; Pages 38-39—vest, Minnesota Historical Society; moccasins, Colter Bay Indian Art Museum; quillwork, photo courtesy of South Dakota State Historical Society–State Archives; porcupine, Grant Heilman, Grant Heilman Photography; quill flattener, Glenbow Collection, Calgary, Alberta (AF 2358); bladder pouch, Dakota Quillwork Sewing Kit, Glenbow Collection, Calgary, Alberta (AF 2389); dress, Brooklyn Museum of Art, 50.67.2; mittens, Brooklyn Museum of Art, 50.67.12a-b; buffalo robe, Yankton Lakota Robe, 1870, gift of the family and friends of Natasha Congdon, 1980.352, Denver Art Museum; woman in robe, Karl Bodmer, Chan-Cha-Uiá-Teüin, Teton Sioux Woman, Joslyn Art Museum, Omaha, NE, gift of the Enron Art Foundation; bandolier bag, Shoulder Bag, ca. 1850, © 1998 The Detroit Institute of Arts; woman and loom, National Museum of the American Indian, Smithsonian Institution;

Chapter Four: Pages 40-41—Swedish keepsakes contents, courtesy of Anna Hamilton; Swedish keepsakes chest, Barbara Johnson Antiques, Rockford, IL; Jultomten, Augustana Book Concern, now Fortress Press Publishers, courtesy American-Swedish News Exchange, Inc.; psalmodiken, hymnal, and bobbin lace, Erlander Home Museum, Rockford, IL; woven cloths, Suzanne Jameson Kramer, Country Gallery Antiques; church, Gammelgården Museum and Park, Scandia, MN; Pages 42-43—Harriet Bishop, Minnesota Historical Society; Yankee and German houses, State Historical Society of Wisconsin's Old World Wisconsin Outdoor Museum; school, State Historical Society of Wisconsin, WHi (X3) 27795; German plate and wood carving, Corbis/Philadelphia Museum of Art; Norwegian cloth and basket, Vesterheim Norwegian-American Museum; picnic, State Historical Society of Wisconsin, WHi (X3) 50622; Pages 44-45—Fourth of July, Corbis/Bettman; growing towns, courtesy of the Oshkosh Public Museum; St. Paul, S. Holmes, Andrews, Minnesota Historical Society; Indians, State Historical Society of Wisconsin, WHi (V2)101;

Chapter Five: Pages 46-47—government supplies, Nah-Koh-Hist (also known as Bear's Heart) *Distribution of Annuities* ca. 1875-1878, pencil, colored pencil, crayon, and colored ink, 97.07.010, National Cowboy Hall of Fame, Oklahoma City, OK; bow and arrow, detail from photograph, courtesy Department of Library Services, American Museum of Natural History, 327 3(4); cut-hairs, photo by Whitney's Gallery, Minnesota Historical Society, E91.7U/rl; cloth dress, State Historical Society of North Dakota, 9969; reservation school, State Historical Society of North Dakota; Civil War poster, Minnesota Historical Society, E425.6/p5; Pages 48-49—Little Crow, photo courtesy of Edward E. Ayer Collection, Newberry Library, Chicago; warbonnet, photographed by John Oldencamp and Cynthia Sabransky, from the David T. Vernon Collection, Colter Bay Indian Arts Museum, Grand Teton National Park, WY; settlers, photo by Adrian Ebell of Whitney's Gallery, Minnesota Historical Society, E91.4S/r20; Fort Snelling, Edward K. Thomas, The Minneapolis Institute of Arts; held captive, Minnesota Historical Society; John Other Day, photo by Whitney, Minnesota Historical Society, E91.1A/r2; Pages 50-51—Mary and Snana, Minnesota Historical Society; rifle, Oregon Historical Society; Pages 52-53—rifle, Oregon Historical Society, ORHi 99162; attacks, by Anton Gag, Minnesota Historical Society; one victory, painting by Anton Gag, Brown County Historical Society, New Ulm, MN; calling the troops, by Stanley Arthurs, Minnesota Historical Society; New Ulm, 1860 Map of New Ulm, by Julius Berndt, Minnesota Historical Society; Dakota books, Minnesota Historical Society; Pages 54-55—taken prisoner, photo by Upton, Minnesota Historical Society, E91.1A/r6; Fort Snelling, photo by Upton, Minnesota Historical Society, E91.4S/p53; family, photo by Upton, Minnesota Historical Society, E91.1L/r20; pushed out, Nebraska State Historical Society, John Anderson Collection; ration card carrier, Ataloa Lodge Museum, Bacone College, Muskogee, OK, photo by Steve Tuttle; ration card, State Historical Society of North Dakota, 663; doll and carrier, Carnegie Museum of Natural History; Sioux girl, South Dakota Department of Tourism; moccasins, "Beaded Tennis Shoes" by Imogene Goodshot (Sioux), is part of the 1985 exhibit "Women of Sweetgrass, Cedar, and Sage: Contemporary Art by Native American Women," curated by Harmony Hammond and Jaune Quick-to-See Smith, photograph courtesy of Atlatl, Inc., National Service Organization for Native American Arts; Pages 56-57—poster, Library of Congress, Rare Books Division; land rush, National Archives (NWDNS-49-AR-7); making tracks, photo courtesy of George A. Poole III Collection, The Newberry Library, Chicago; beauty in a harsh land, Wyoming Division of Cultural Resources; natural wonders, *Tower Falls* by Thomas Moran, 1872, watercolor on paper, 0226.1457, from the collection of Gilcrease Museum, Tulsa, OK.

Table of Contents

Welcome to Kirsten's World

Kirsten tried to imagine a farm right next door to her new cousins. She hoped this American home would be just like the one she left in Sweden, with the maple tree by the door.

—Meet Kirsten

♥

Wherever Kirsten went in her small town of Ryd (reed) in Sweden, there was one word on everyone's lips: *America!* America was the New World, many said, and Sweden was the old. In America everything was possible. *"The land is plentiful,"* said the booklets about this new country. *"The cattle are the finest in the world. . . . There are fruit trees everywhere. . . . Everyone who works hard can have his own farm."*

Ordinary farm families packed up all their belongings and sailed to America. Then Swedes like Uncle Olav wrote to family and friends back in Sweden from their new farms in Wisconsin, Minnesota, and Iowa. "Come join us," the letters said.

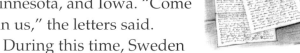

During this time, Sweden had so many people that there weren't enough farms for everyone. Sweden's king decided to divide each farm in half, so twice as many families could have land. But that only made the problem worse. Each farm was too small to grow enough food. Many families were only one bad harvest away from starvation.

Going to America made good sense. The New World was a place where families could build a new and better life. Many Swedes, just like the Larsons, decided to do just that.

Saying Good-Bye

Many Swedish families sold their farms, oxen, horses, and chickens and purchased tickets to America. Then they brought the big clothes trunk down from the loft and scrubbed and polished it. The whole family had to fit their most important things into one trunk. And everyone in the village had advice about what to pack in the "America chest."

Powder horn

Spinning wheel

Copper kettle

America chest

1844 KOD

Carpentry drill

Lantern

Carpenter's plane to shave wood boards

Woven crib blanket

Wooden container, called a **tine** (TEE-na)

For the long crossing, family members carried food and supplies
in knapsacks, bundles. and baskets.

Family Bible

*An immigrant girl
carried her kitten all
the way to America
in this basket.*

TOYS
If a child like Kirsten
was lucky, she might
have a doll or toy in
her bundle to play
with during the
long trip.

A Final Good-Bye

By sunup on the day a family left for
America, a flatbed wagon stood waiting
at the cottage door. Grandparents
hugged their sons and daughters and
held the little ones close. All along the
rutted dirt road, people heard the sound
of the wagon and ran to their doors to
wave. They knew someone was leaving
for America, and they wanted to bid a
last farewell.

　　Most Swedes had never seen the sea
before. They were people of the land
who had never felt the rising and falling
of ocean waves under their feet. Their
first steps on board ship were awkward,
and they grabbed at the railing, afraid
to let go.

　　When storms rocked their ship from
side to side, Mama calmed
Kirsten with stories
about Uncle Olav,
his new family,
and his farm in
America. Mama's
words swirled in
Kirsten's head as she
tried to imagine her new home.
　　Little by little, this mysterious
country on a distant shore
began to take shape in her mind.

The Journey

It took at least six weeks for Kirsten and her family to sail across the Atlantic Ocean. As Kirsten's ship sailed into New York Harbor, the passengers were astonished at the number of other ships, both large and small, already in the narrow waters.

Each day, immigrants from all over Europe were leaving the troubles of their homelands behind them. In 1845, Ireland's potato crop failed. By 1848, a million Irish people had starved to death and another million had left for America. That same year, some Germans rebelled against their government and lost. Many fled to America rather than face prison or death.

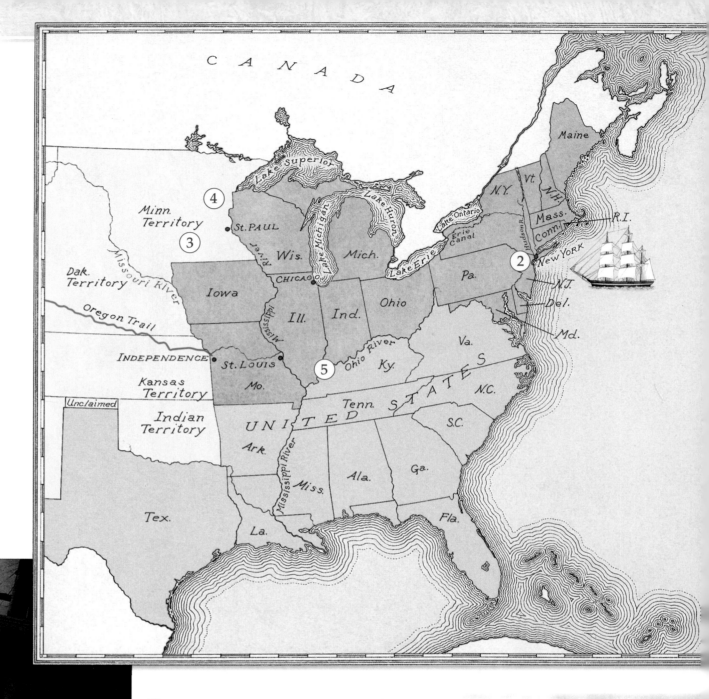

① SAILING FOR AMERICA
In 1854, many Swedes sailed for America on cargo ships. Passengers stayed on deck as much as possible—even in rough weather. Otherwise, they had to crowd into the windowless, foul-smelling *steerage compartment* at the bottom of the ship near the steering equipment.

ATLANTIC OCEAN

N
W E
S

LEGEND

☐ *Frontier*
▨ *Northern States*
☐ *Southern States*

⑤ A NATION DIVIDED

By 1850, the North ended slavery, but the South kept it legal. Most Northerners chose to overlook slavery in the South. Then in 1852, Harriet Beecher Stowe wrote the book *Uncle Tom's Cabin.* This book made Northerners realize how cruel slavery was and further divided the North and South. Eventually this division led to the Civil War.

④ NATIVE AMERICANS

The Dakota Sioux (soo) and the Ojibway (oh-JIB-way) Indians had long lived on the land that made up the Minnesota Territory. In 1851, the U.S. had signed treaties with the Indians, promising them money for their land. However, the U.S. didn't pay the Indians on time. It was too late for the Indians to take back their land. The settlers were already flooding into Minnesota to farm its rich soil.

② NEW YORK CITY

Each month, thousands of immigrants from Europe arrived in New York City. For some, New York City became their new home. For others, like the Larsons, the city was only the beginning of their journey in America.

③ THE FRONTIER

Kirsten's new home was on America's *frontier*—land that was mostly unsettled by whites. By 1854, thousands of white settlers were moving farther west. They drove their covered wagons along the Oregon Trail to the West Coast. They panned for gold or worked in logging camps over the winter to earn money.

America at Last

Kirsten worried that the health inspector wouldn't let Mama into America because she'd been sick. But Mama had only been seasick. She didn't have a disease that killed people. Health inspectors looked for passengers who had the severe stomach cramps of *cholera* (KAH-ler-uh) or the red rash of *typhus* (TY-fus). If even one passenger had a deadly disease, the whole ship was *quarantined* (KWOR-an-teened), or kept away from shore and other ships. The quarantine could last for weeks, and some ships were even sent back to Europe.

If everyone on board was healthy, the ship was allowed to dock in New York Harbor. Imagine how strange Kirsten must have felt when she stepped off the ship and set foot in New York City—the busiest, most bustling port in America.

New York had the tallest buildings many immigrants had ever seen.

*The sign for the shop selling **nautical,** or sailing, instruments was shaped to look like a sextant. A sextant was a tool to help sailors chart their course.*

The first thing immigrants did when they got off the boat was find a bank to exchange their money for American money.

① CASTLE GARDEN
When the Larsons came to America, they just walked off the ship and continued on their journey. The next year Castle Garden opened. It was America's first immigration station. In 1892, Castle Garden closed and a larger station opened on nearby Ellis Island.

② STOREFRONTS
Fish markets, sail makers, and trading companies all had storefronts along the docks. Ticket agents sold railroad, stagecoach, and riverboat tickets from their offices.

③ SWINDLERS
Some people made their living by *swindling,* or cheating, newcomers. They sold train tickets to nowhere and booked hotel rooms that didn't exist. Booklets warned immigrants not to trust agents who eagerly swarmed around them.

After so many weeks on board the cramped ship, children couldn't wait to run and play.

④ COBBLESTONE CLATTER
Hundreds of carts and horses lined the waterfront, waiting to load cargo from the ships. The clatter of horse hooves and ironclad wheels on cobblestones made a constant racket.

⑧ Ships
Packet ships carried packages, or cargo, and immigrants. Packet ships were the first ships to sail on a regular schedule. This made it easier for immigrants to plan their arrival in America.

⑦ Captain
The ship's captain sometimes helped immigrants exchange money, find nearby boarding houses, and buy train tickets west.

⑥ Buggy Luggage
Before the trunks could be taken off a ship, they sometimes had to be *fumigated* (FYOO-muh-gay-ted), or sprayed with a gas that killed bugs.

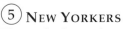

⑤ New Yorkers
Elegantly dressed men and women came to meet first-class passengers. One British visitor thought New York women looked like a "moving bed of tulips."

People chattered and shouted in many different languages.

West to *Chicago*

After resting for the night in a New York boarding house, Kirsten's family was ready to start their long journey to Chicago. Marta's family, however, would not begin their journey until the next day. The two families were both going to Chicago, but they were taking different routes. No one could guess how long the trips would take. Kirsten and Marta worried that they might never see each other again.

SWEDE TOWN
When Swedish immigrants reached Chicago, they stayed in an area known as Swede Town. Kirsten and Marta were reunited when they stayed at a boarding house there.

① TRAIN TRAVEL
Kirsten's family took the train to Chicago. Passengers had to change trains several times. For each change, they dragged their heavy trunks from one train to the next.

② HUDSON RIVER STEAMBOAT
Marta and her family took a steamboat to Albany, New York. They traveled in "immigrant class," on the lower deck. There was often standing room only, even overnight.

From the book Meet Kirsten

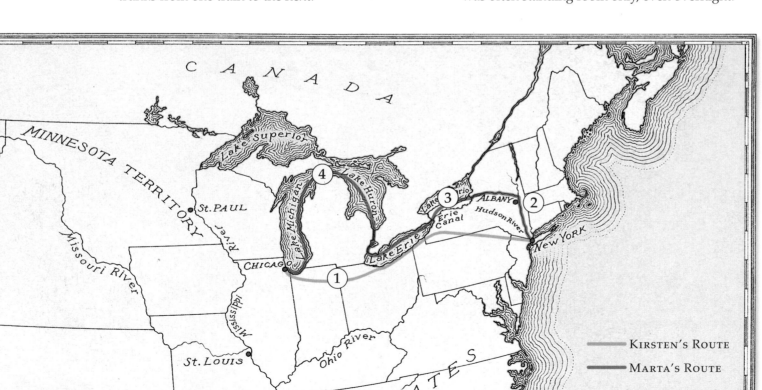

③ CANAL BOATS
A canal boat took Marta's family through the Erie Canal. Immigrants' trunks and bundles of household goods were tied to the decks.

④ GREAT LAKES STEAMER
Finally, Marta's family took a steamboat across Lake Erie, Lake Huron, and Lake Michigan to reach Chicago.

KIRSTEN'S ROUTE
MARTA'S ROUTE

*By 1855, Chicago had a Swedish-language newspaper, the **Hemlandet**, or homeland.*

Swedish immigrants kept precious letters from their homeland with them on their journey.

STREETS OF CHICAGO
In 1854, there was no mistaking Chicago for New York City. Stone was hard to get in Chicago, so the buildings were made of wood and the streets were not paved. Every street, however, had wide wooden sidewalks and footpaths for crossing. Without them, these girls would be ankle deep in mud!

Residents placed funny signs at particularly muddy spots.

BUSINESS IS BOOMING
By the 1850s, new railroads were turning the frontier town of Chicago into a bustling city. Trains brought merchants more goods than ever before.

The first cobblestone streets were laid in Chicago in 1857.

Mississippi Riverboat

From the moment Kirsten saw the Mississippi riverboat, she couldn't wait for it to take her to Minnesota. Finally, she and her family were on the last leg of their journey.

In 1854, the Mississippi River was America's highway. It was full of riverboats—some plain, some as fancy as wedding cakes. They traveled all the way from New Orleans to Minnesota and back.

① COUNTRYSIDE
As the riverboat pushed its way up the Mississippi, passengers saw flat farmland, steep bluffs, and trees they'd never seen before.

② INDIANS
Passengers sometimes saw Dakota or Ojibway Indians watching the riverboats.

③ FRESH AIR
During the heat of summer, some Southerners headed north to Minnesota, where the air was free of diseases like malaria and yellow fever, which thrived in the hot and humid South.

④ UPPER DECK
While a band played, wealthy southern planters escorted their ladies around the upper deck. They enjoyed their own private rooms and spent their afternoons taking tea or playing cards.

⑤ MAIN DECK
The main deck was a crowded jumble of immigrants, Easterners, and adventurers, all looking for new lives.

⑥ DRINKING WATER
To take a drink of water out of the barrel, passengers had to brush away the flies that gathered on its edges.

⑦ SLAVES
The black slaves of the wealthy Southerners traveled on the main deck, shackled together.

A Sad Stop

When Marta became sick, there was nothing Kirsten could do. When a passenger died, the riverboat stopped so the dead could be buried onshore.

"A bell rang on the upper deck, the steering wheel turned. . . . The boat moored to a lonely bank deep in the forest. . . . The gangplank was thrown out, and two of the crewmen went on shore carrying an oblong bundle between them. . . . After a short while the men returned to the ship. But now they carried nothing except the shovels dangling in their hands. . . ."

—The Emigrants *by Vilhelm Moberg*

(8) **TOBACCO**
If a *spittoon*, or bucket, wasn't provided, the men spit so much tobacco on the floor that the women had to hold up their skirts as they walked across it.

(9) **DISEASE**
The filthy conditions on the main deck led to outbreaks of deadly cholera and typhus, which spread from passenger to passenger.

New Home

Kirsten was happy to get off the riverboat and finally set foot in Minnesota. The Larsons, like all the other new immigrants, had been idle during the long weeks of their journey to America. Now they itched to begin the hard work of plowing and planting their new farms. There wasn't a moment to waste as they started to build new homes—and new lives—on the Minnesota frontier.

In Sweden, log cabins were made from pine trees. The Minnesota woods were full of pines, maples, and oaks.

This saw was fashioned from a birch branch and a metal blade.

1. CLEARING THE LAND
Settlers from neighboring farms held logging bees to help newcomers clear their land. They used felled trees to build log cabins.

A large stump could take all day to grub out of the ground.

2. GRUBBING THE STUMPS
Once the trees were cleared, the men and older boys used hoes and axes to *grub*, or dig, stubborn stumps out of the ground. Women and children helped, too, by pulling up the roots.

Axe for chopping, notching, and grubbing

A family's first log cabin was very small. Settlers needed to use their early months in America to plant and harvest their first crop.

4. LIFTING LOGS
Neighbors helped newcomers build cabins, too. Five men might need four full days to finish a one-room cabin. Together they lifted the heavy logs on top of one another to form the walls.

3. PREPARING LOGS
Men made *notches*, or deep cuts, in the logs so they would fit together tightly. The bark was stripped off the logs before building.

5. DAUBING WITH MUD
Once the roof was on, women and older children filled the cracks between the logs with mud.

Daubing was also called **chinking.** *Chinking material could be mud, moss, clay, or mortar.*

Wooden bucket for mixing chinking material

6. PLANTING
A farmer might grow potatoes or wheat in his plowed field. Nearer the cabin, his wife and children tended a kitchen garden full of vegetables and herbs. They also planted flowers to make their new house feel like home.

A Wonderful Sight

After so many weeks and months squeezed into crowded ships, trains, and riverboats, a finished log cabin—even one with just a single room—was a wonderful sight. No matter how tiny the new house might be, it seemed big enough to hold the dreams of an entire family.

The cabin's door was little more than rough boards held together with wooden pegs and hung on leather or wooden hinges. Glass was expensive and scarce, so paper usually covered the one small window. Settlers often greased the paper so it would let in more light.

The entire family looked forward to the day when the cabin was finished and the America chest could be brought inside and opened. Out came the handwoven linens and rugs, brass candlesticks, and copper pots. The colorful patterns and bright shiny objects from Sweden made the simple log cabin feel like a true home in America.

Prairie Homes

Kirsten saw many kinds of homes on the Minnesota frontier. She lived in an area where there were enough trees to make houses and barns from wood. Dakota and Ojibway Indians lived nearby in tepees and wigwams. Farther west, on the flat prairie, houses were made from clumps of dirt and grass, called *sod*.

Canvas sides rolled up to let fresh air in.

PRAIRIE SCHOONERS
At first, new settlers lived in their covered wagons, also called *prairie schooners*. The white canvas covers reminded people of the sails on schooners, a type of ship.

The roof could hold the weight of horses and a wagon. The wagon is filled with sod to repair the roof.

FRAME HOUSES
Successful settlers built clapboard farmhouses. They often turned their old cabins or soddies into stables.

SODDIES
Some homes were built with sod bricks made of grass and earth. This soddie was dug into the side of a small hill.

A built-in swing.

When people or animals walked on the roof, dirt fell inside.

A heavy rain turned the floor into a muddy mess. It also brought insects and snakes inside!

Summer wildflowers bloomed on the roofs of sod houses.

TEPEE ORNAMENTS

The Dakota liked to attach ornaments to the tops of tepee poles and door flaps.

The rattling of these hooves announced the arrival of a visitor.

Decorated leather thongs

INDIAN SUMMER HOMES

Dakota and Ojibway Indians moved from place to place. During the summer, they lived in long homes made with poles and bark. These large homes let in more cool air, and the heat rose up through the high roof.

DAKOTA TEPEES

In the winter, the Dakota lived in tepees. They were quick to set up and take down, and their smaller size kept families snug for the winter.

Sawmills cut logs into boards for clapboard siding.

OJIBWAY WIGWAMS

In the winter, the Ojibway lived in wigwams made of birch bark. They overlapped the bark pieces and put layers of moss in between for warmth.

Fun T*i*mes

Pioneers had little time for fun, but sometimes they turned their work into a party. Whenever there was a big job to be completed in a short time, they invited neighbors to a special work party called a *bee*. Bees were held to husk corn, build houses or barns, or sew quilts. There was always plenty of food, music, and sometimes dancing, too—when the work was finished, of course!

BARN RAISING
The old expression "many hands make light work" was especially true when it came to building a house or barn. Neighbors needed each other and rarely turned down a call for help.

Pioneer women would blow on a hollow cow horn to call workers in for dinner.

QUILTING BEES
These gatherings gave farm women a chance to trade stories and share news. When they finished the quilt, they needed to test its strength. Sometimes the smallest child climbed on top and was tossed gently into the air.

SCUTCHING BEES
Pioneer men and women also held scutching bees. They used scutching knives to *scutch*, or beat the fibers from, flax plants. Then the fibers were spun into linen thread and woven into cloth.

After the work, there was time for play. Here, the women are trying to knock off the men's hats with their scutching knives!

CORNHUSKING BEES
At harvest time, everyone gathered to husk corn. If a man found a colored ear of corn, he was permitted to kiss the lady of his choice!

Piano accordion

Key fiddle

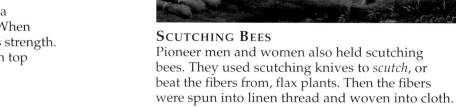

BARN DANCING
At the end of any bee, people brought out the instruments and the music began.

From the book *Happy Birthday, Kirsten!*

Sparking

Hardworking settlers were the first to agree that life on the frontier needed the "spark" of a courtship. So courting was also called *sparking*. An entire community took notice when romance was in the air. But in areas where farms were miles apart, it wasn't easy for young men and women to meet. When a barn dance or a bee was planned, men rode the countryside looking for new settlers to invite— especially those who might have a pretty daughter or two. Some gatherings were held just so men could meet the new arrivals and begin sparking!

COUNTRY DANCES
Many settlers met at country dances, or *sprees*. Couples jigged, reeled, and square-danced to lively fiddle music, sometimes until dawn!

COURTSHIP GIFTS
A man might give a richly decorated tool for the home as a courtship gift. The more beautiful the decoration, the more in love the young man was!

*This scutching knife is decorated with **rosemaling**, a popular Scandinavian painting style.*

Women held on to a mangle's handle and ran the bottom over damp clothes to smooth them.

VALENTINES
Many pioneers made their valentines by hand. Books called *valentine writers* helped them find funny and romantic verses for their sweethearts.

*Women wound wool or flax fibers around the carved end of a **distaff**. Then they spun the fibers into thread.*

Swedish girls were told to "beware of the man with too many mangles." If he had lots of mangles, he had courted and been refused many times!

BETROTHAL CHEST

Engaged Swedish couples followed many of the traditions of their homeland. After a young man's proposal was accepted, he might make a betrothal chest and fill it with small presents, such as a hymnal, gloves, or a shawl for his beloved.

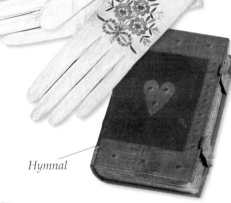

Hymnal

COURTING BLANKETS

Young people in Indian tribes courted, too. Courting couples in the Cheyenne and Dakota tribes wrapped themselves in double blankets when they wanted to speak in private.

A Dakota man played love songs on a courting flute to win a young woman's affection.

SLEIGH RIDING

In 1860, a Nebraska newspaper commented on the pastimes of courting couples. A boy would collect a "toll"—a kiss—from the girl next to him every time their sleigh or wagon crossed a bridge. Sometimes a couple crossed the same bridge over and over again!

ENGAGEMENT PICTURE

This couple took an entire day off from their farm chores to ride into town and have an engagement portrait taken. They sent it to friends and family back home in Sweden.

eddings

One pioneer man worked so hard that he barely left his chores long enough to marry his beloved! When his wedding day arrived, he noted:

"In the morning . . . chopped cornstalks. At noon . . . started plowing. . . . In the evening at 5 o'clock Elsa's and my expectations became a reality, a marriage."

MINISTER'S CHEST

Many early communities didn't have their own churches, so they shared a minister. Inside his traveling chest, he kept his Bible and other religious objects.

SUITORS' SPOONS

A *suitor* is a man who courts a woman. Suitors' spoons were placed before the bride and groom at the wedding feast as a joke— they were impossible to eat with!

WEDDINGS

Weddings on the frontier often took place between Christmas and New Year's. Because there was no planting or harvesting to do, farm families had time to celebrate.

Whole communities were invited to Swedish weddings.

This Swedish bride's crown was made with leaves, flowers, and vines.

WEDDING BELLS

Some couples preferred to keep their wedding a secret. If neighbors found out, they serenaded the couple with the unmusical sounds of cowbells and sleigh bells.

BRIDAL CROWN

Swedish brides were crowned queen for a day on their wedding day. The family bridal crown, or *brudkrona* (brood-KROO-nah), could be one foot high!

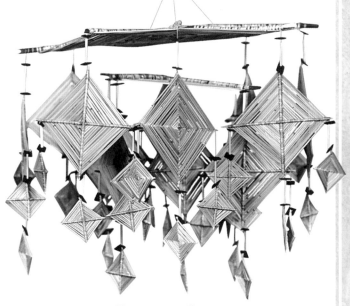

HANGING CROWN

A fancy crown made out of wood and straw was hung from the ceiling above a Swedish bride's place at the table. The heat from candles set underneath made the crown spin slowly.

WEDDING BASKET

Guests brought wedding baskets filled with flowers or baked goods to help celebrate.

GREEN GOWNS

On the prairie, wedding gowns were rarely white. Women usually wore their best dresses. Norwegian brides favored green gowns because the color reminded them of home. Green was a popular color in Norwegian folk costumes.

Daily Life on the Homestead

Pioneer families came to America ready to work. Yet even the heartiest weren't prepared for the endless chores that turned a *homestead*—the cabin and the land surrounding it—into a farm. The first year was spent clearing the land, building the barn and cabin, and planting the crops. Then the everyday work of running the home and the farm could begin.

As the settlers farmed their land, they met the Indians who lived nearby. Some were frightened of the Indians and didn't want them near their farms. But others became friends with them. Indians taught settlers how to track animals and which herbs and barks would keep their families healthy. In return, the settlers shared their harvests.

① SOAP MAKING
To make soap, women mixed *lye*, made from rainwater and fireplace ashes, with *lard*, or hog fat. The mixture became a thick jelly used to wash dishes and laundry.

② WATCH THE FIRE!
Children kept a close watch on the fire. If the fire went out, it was their job to walk miles to the nearest neighbor's farm and carry hot coals in a tin pail all the way back.

③ OUTHOUSE
Settlers used dried cornhusks or leaves as toilet paper.

Flax

④ SPINNING
Women used a spinning wheel to spin wool into yarn and flax into thread.

⑤ MILK TO CREAM TO BUTTER
After milk sat awhile, the cream rose to the surface. Girls skimmed it off and churned the cream until it separated into buttermilk and solid pellets of butter.

Even everyday objects like this rake were decorated with rosemaling.

⑫ BARN

Barns were built in a hurry to protect the family's animals, grain, and tools during the first long winter. After a few growing seasons, farmers made their barns much larger and stronger.

⑪ PLOWING FIELDS

Settlers used oxen and a heavy plow to loosen the soil for planting. They scattered the seeds in the fields with a *harrow*, or a large rake, then the oxen dragged earth over them.

⑩ DAIRY COW

Children helped keep the family's dairy cow from grazing on strong-tasting plants like wild onions or garlic. If the cow ate those plants, the milk would taste terrible!

⑨ CHICKENS

Chickens were important for their meat and eggs, but they could be troublesome. Children shooed chickens out of the fields so they wouldn't eat the family's grain.

⑧ PUMPKINS

Indians taught the earliest settlers that pumpkin vines helped smother weeds that grew around corn and other valuable crops.

⑥ HAULING WATER

Pioneer homes didn't have running water, so water had to be hauled from a nearby stream.

⑦ FLOWERS

Many Swedish settlers brought daylily, bleeding heart, and aster seeds with them from their homeland.

Daylilies

Daily Life of the Dakota

Singing Bird's people, the Dakota, believed that land was for everyone to share. But white settlers had different ideas. They moved onto the land and built homes and fences. They called the land theirs. All of the building and activity chased away the wild animals the Dakota needed for food.

In 1851, the U.S. government offered the Dakota a treaty. The government would give the Dakota money and food for the land they lived on in Minnesota. In return, the Dakota would move to a *reservation*, or land set aside for them. Singing Bird's people were starving. They had no choice but to sign the treaty. They had lost their homeland, but they still held on to their way of life.

① SUMMER HOMES
Dakota summer homes were located near land that was good for hunting and fishing. They built large houses from wood and bark, and several families lived together.

The Dakota burned braids of sweet grass for its pleasant scent.

② DRYING RACKS
These tall racks kept supplies safe from wild animals. Also, hides, corn, and meat dried faster high above the roofs of the summer houses.

③ DOGS
The Dakota kept many dogs for protection and hunting.

④ IRON KETTLES
Traders brought iron kettles to the Dakota. Before that, food had to be cooked in bark containers.

⑤ SANDY SOIL
Summer homes were usually built on soft, sandy soil so their poles could be driven in easily.

(11) SCAFFOLDS
Scaffolds, or tall platforms, provided shade during a hot summer day, and a cool place to sleep at night.

This scraper is made from an elk horn.

(10) ANIMAL HIDES
Indians used animal skins to make both clothing and shelter. To make leather, women stretched the hides on racks to dry. Then they cleaned and softened the hides with scrapers.

(9) PLAYTIME
As boys played with small bows and arrows, they began to learn the skills needed by men. Girls imitated their mothers by playing with buckskin dolls and tiny tepees.

(6) SUMMER HUNT
The Dakota were not farmers. They usually planted only small plots of corn and squash. Their main source of food came from hunting deer, elk, and buffalo in the summer.

(7) CRADLEBOARDS
Babies spent most of their first year in portable cradles. Cradleboards were made from wood, and animal skins or canvas. The insides were padded with moss or shredded bark.

(8) SEWING
Women sewed moccasins and clothes out of leather. They decorated them with dyed porcupine quills and beads.

25

Living by the Seasons

Both the pioneers and the Indians lived according to the changing of the seasons. Their year began not on January 1, but with the first buds of spring. Then both settler and Indian families began the cycle of work that ended when the snow and cold returned.

SPRING

As soon as the spring sun warmed the earth, settlers began to plow and plant. The Dakota and Ojibway Indians moved near newly thawed streams to hunt and fish.

CORN
Women and children helped by planting corn. They put six corn kernels in each hole because they knew some wouldn't sprout.

BUILDING CANOES
Fishing was best in the springtime, just as streams, rivers, and lakes began to thaw. Indians made birch bark canoes that moved silently through the water.

MAPLE SUGAR
Ojibway boys and girls tapped the maple trees and collected their sap. Then the sap was boiled down into syrup. If there was lots of syrup, children dropped spoonfuls of it into the snow. It hardened into candy!

SUMMER

Settlers tended their crops and watched their livestock grow fat. Families couldn't spare much time away from the fields, so picnics or barn raisings were a rare treat. The Dakota moved to their bark homes, which were cooler and better ventilated. There they planted gardens, picked berries, and hunted.

HAY HARVEST
The whole family helped bring in the hay that would feed their animals for the year. This job was done in the hottest weather so the hay was dry for storing.

BUFFALO HUNT
Buffalo were not as plentiful in Minnesota as they were farther west, but hunts were still held every summer.

GOOD TIMES
After a successful hunt, the Dakota had ceremonies, dances, and ball games. Neighboring tribes came to challenge the Dakota men in *lacrosse*, one of their favorite ball games.

FALL

When the winds began to blow the leaves off the trees, everyone knew winter was near. Settlers hurried their harvest and preserved the summer's fruits and vegetables. Dakota men and boys hunted while the good weather lasted. When they returned, the women dried the meat and tanned the hides.

APPLE HARVEST
Women carefully packed and stored the best apples for winter eating. The rest were pressed into cider or vinegar, cooked down to make apple sauce and apple butter, or cut into rings and dried.

PRESERVING MEAT
Settlers butchered hogs so the family had meat for the year. They cleaned the carcasses, then salted or smoked the meat to preserve it.

RICE GATHERING
The Ojibway slowly paddled their birch bark canoes through marshes and gathered wild rice. Women bent the tall stalks and beat the seed heads with sticks until the bottom of the canoe was full of rice.

WINTER

During the winter, both the Indians and the settlers had time to catch up on repair jobs. The Dakota set up tepees in the shelter of trees. Settlers worked in their homes and outbuildings.

QUIET TASKS
Dakota women made clothes, mended snowshoes, and told stories around the warm fire in the center of the tepee while the men hunted on snowshoes.

REPAIRS
Settler men fixed plows, carts, and other tools. Women took advantage of the quiet days to mend old clothes and make new ones.

Grasshoppers!

A pioneer's life was difficult enough, but extreme changes in the weather made it even more dangerous and uncertain. Blizzards, hail, tornadoes, and lightning all damaged cabins and farms. But grasshopper swarms were the most destructive of all.

What a sight when we opened the door! The sky was darkened by grasshoppers. Everything in that lovely garden was gone... the wheat fields looked as if they had been burned... not a leaf on the trees.
— a Minnesota pioneer, 1856

The hoppers, as they were called, would come every summer for several years and then stop. Ten or 20 years later, they would return again. No one understood what brought on a hopper plague, but it caused farmers to lose everything.

Desperate farmers watched as the hoppers ate a year's worth of crops in a day. And the next year, the hoppers returned to do the same thing. One Swedish woman wrote home, "*It is sad and distressing and depressing for body and soul to find that no matter how hard one drudges and works, one still has nothing less than nothing.*"

In Kirsten's time there were no pesticides to kill the grasshoppers, so farmers tried plowing them under the soil, catching them in wire nets, dipping them in kerosene, or burning them. Most methods did not work or worked only for a while. Sooner or later, the hoppers would come back.

Med*i*cine

Weather changes and grasshopper plagues weren't the only difficulties pioneers had to face. They also had to survive illnesses when there were few doctors to call for help. Women like Mama tried to keep their families healthy by using home remedies. When they could, they called a doctor. But often doctors could not make people well either. Pioneer medicine was very basic, and even doctors didn't know that germs caused many diseases.

Doctors carried medical kits in their saddlebags.

DOCTOR'S SAW
Farming caused many accidents. If a farmer badly injured his arm or leg, a doctor might have to *amputate*, or saw off, the limb in order to save his life.

DOCTOR ON HORSEBACK
A frontier doctor rode on horseback or in a buggy to answer calls. He would come at any time of the day or night, and he even traveled through blizzards!

STETHOSCOPE
In the 1850s, equipment like this *stethoscope*, used to listen to heartbeats, let doctors know what was happening inside the body.

PIONEER DOCTORS
Most pioneer doctors used their hands, ears, and eyes to *diagnose* (dye-ig-NOHS), or recognize symptoms of, diseases. In the 1850s, doctors were just beginning to learn how to measure a patient's pulse, temperature, and blood pressure.

MARK'S CELEBRATED ME

MEDICINES

Some pioneers had their own medicine chests. They bought tonics or medicines from a doctor or peddler, or they ground and mixed herbs to make their own medicines.

ILLNESS AND EPIDEMICS

In prairie communities an *epidemic*, or outbreak of a disease such as smallpox, often took the lives of small children. These parents are at the grave of their 19-month-old son.

RECEIPT BOOK

Women turned to their *receipt*, or recipe, books to find cures for common illnesses.

MEDICINE WAGON

Peter Mark was a Minnesota druggist who took his drugstore on the road. Children ran after his wagon because he gave out gum and candy if their parents bought his medicine.

MEDICINE WHEEL

For the Dakota, the medicine wheel symbolized a balanced, healthy life. They imagined themselves balancing in the middle of the wheel.

Fuzzy cattail down was used to treat burns.

NATIVE AMERICAN HEALING

The Dakota and Ojibway Indians taught the settlers how to use roots, bulbs, herbs, berries, and seeds for healing. The Indians chewed prickly-ash bark to ease toothaches and drank gumweed tea for coughs.

NO 6

DICINES.

Settler Childhood

Pioneer girls and boys spent most of their time working at the same kinds of jobs their parents did. Girls helped their mothers in the house and boys helped their fathers on the farm. Children attended school only when they weren't needed at home. Even though they were busy, pioneer children still found ways to have fun. They made lots of their own toys and found things to play with in the meadows and woods.

An open milkweed pod made a perfect fairy cradle, and the fluffy silk became a tiny pillow.

*Children played with this chromatrope toy by spinning it. **Chroma** means colors, and **trope** means turn.*

PAPER DOLLS
Some store-bought paper dolls came with names and stories so girls could act out their favorite parts.

RAG DOLLS
Girls learned how to sew by making dresses and bonnets for their rag dolls.

Girls who lived in town didn't have as many chores as farm girls. They had time to make decorative samplers to show their fine stitches.

CHILDREN'S CHORES
When settler children were about four years old, they took on chores like feeding the chickens, gathering eggs, and carrying water.

Books were scarce. Some teachers used their family Bible to teach reading.

Outdoor Games

At recess, children played games you might play today—Tree Tag, Fox and Geese, and Puss in the Corner. These boys are playing Crack the Whip.

School

Most pioneer children attended school in winter and summer. During spring and fall, they helped their families on the farm.

Children kept their skates on by tying leather thongs around their boots.

Some girls as young as six years old learned how to knit caps and mittens.

Winter Fun

In the winter, children went sledding and skating. They held contests to see who could slide down the hill or skate across the ice the fastest!

Peg in the Ring

To play Peg in the Ring, children spun tops in a circle on the ground. If one player's top hit another, that player kept both tops!

Native American Childhood

Dakota children were adored by their families and given many toys. By Singing Bird's time, they had Ojibway toys, too. The tribes often traded with each other.

Until Dakota children were six, they were allowed to run and play without worrying about chores. But young children still had lessons to learn. They had to be quiet and still when asked only once. During times of danger, sudden noise or movement threatened the entire tribe. Children also learned that lying brought great dishonor and was punished. Parents rarely hit their children, though. They believed it would harm a child's spirit.

TURTLE CHARMS
Often new babies were given two beaded turtles. One held the baby's umbilical cord, which was a symbol of life. The other was empty to confuse any spirits trying to steal the baby's life.

Girls made doll dresses and moccasins in the style of the tribe.

Women strapped cradleboards on their backs, like backpacks.

The doll in this cradleboard came from European traders.

The wooden hoop protected the baby's head. The dangling charms kept her entertained.

INDIAN DOLLS
Grandmothers often made dolls for their granddaughters. They made the dolls without facial features, and then the girls gave the dolls faces and personalities.

THE "THIRD MOTHER"
Ojibway believed the first people came from the earth, their "first mother." Human mothers were "second mothers." Cradleboards were "third mothers" because they protected babies and held them close.

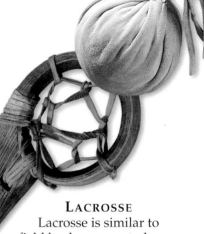

LACROSSE

Lacrosse is similar to field hockey, except players throw and catch a ball instead of striking it along the ground. It taught children swiftness and sharpness of the eye.

GAMES

When older Dakota children weren't working, they played ball games, ran races, held jumping and shooting contests, and played guessing games indoors. These boys are playing Follow the Leader.

HOUSEHOLD SKILLS

By the time girls were ten, they knew how to cook, sew, tan hides, quill, and bead. One Dakota woman explained, "A girl who helped the grown-ups was much honored."

These moccasins were worn only for special occasions

MOCCASINS

At age seven or eight, a Dakota girl made her first pair of moccasins. If she gave them to an older brother, he became her protector in exchange.

RING AND PIN GAME

In this game, players held the metal pin pointing up and let the deer bones hang down. Then they swung the string and tried to catch the bones on the pin.

TINY TEPEES

Dakota girls practiced their homemaking skills by making tiny tepees for their dolls.

TOY CANOE

Parents thought that if children played with a properly made toy canoe, they would understand how to build a full-sized one someday.

35

Settler Fashion

Pioneers like Kirsten and Mama only had a few simple dresses. They wove wool or linen cloth themselves or bought *calico*, or cheap cotton cloth, in town. Then they sewed the dresses by hand. Their dresses had to be practical because they worked in them every day. Some pioneer women had a finer dress brought from the east or from their homeland. But on the prairie, best dresses were worn only for special occasions.

*A braid pinned to the top of the head was called a **cat** because it curled over a girl's head like a cat.*

Collars were removable for easy washing.

HOOPS
Hoops held out the skirts of fancy dresses. They were made of steel and cotton and tied around the waist.

Coral beads and gold charms

GIRLS' DRESSES
Young girls wore dresses that ended just below their knees. The shorter skirts made it easier to run and play.

Girls tried hard to keep their pantalettes snowy white, even on the dusty prairie.

This skirt gets its pouf from a hoop.

SUNDAY BEST
These sisters wore their best dresses and jewelry to pose for a photograph.

"Grow stripes" were let out as girls grew taller.

SUNBONNET
Sunbonnets kept pioneer women from getting sunburns or suntans, which were considered very unladylike.

A Swedish birch bark purse

HAIR JEWELRY
Women braided locks of their hair into necklaces, earrings, and bracelets.

PETTICOATS
Quilted petticoats were thick and warm on the cold prairie.

Silk fabric and fringe trims were imported all the way from France.

FASHIONABLE DRESSES
Women read fashion magazines to keep up on the latest dress styles.

CHATELAINE
Some women wore a *chatelaine* (SHAT-uh-lane) at the waist. It kept sewing equipment, such as thimbles or needles, close at hand.

CORSET AND CHEMISE
A woman wore a corset to help support and shape the body. Underneath, she wore a *chemise* (sheh-MEEZ), or knee-length undershirt.

Cotton stockings reached just above the knee.

Chemises were decorated with delicate embroidery.

Handmade leather boots

Steel rods made corsets stiff.

Native American Dress

Dakota women and girls made all of the clothes for themselves and their families. They tanned animal hides to make robes, dresses, shirts, leggings, and moccasins. Then they decorated the clothes with paints, quills, feathers, and shells. Glass beads from European traders were also used for beadwork and jewelry.

The color yellow meant maturity. Perhaps the child was just beginning to act grown up.

QUILLWORK
Women and girls sorted and dyed porcupine quills and softened them by sucking on them. Then they flattened the quills and sewed them onto animal hides.

Dakota men threw blankets over porcupines and collected the quills that stuck to the blankets.

Women pressed the flat side of this hook over quills to flatten them.

Buffalo bladder pouch for storing quills

Quills colored with root and vegetable dyes

Undyed porcupine quills

BUFFALO ROBE

Dakota women painted designs on buffalo robes. On men's robes they painted horses or buffalo, which meant good hunting. On their own robes, they painted geometric designs.

The color red meant life.

The color blue meant peace and **tranquillity***, or calm.*

A paintbrush made by tying animal hair to the end of a stick

The Ojibway sewed flower patterns that they saw in the woods and fields.

OJIBWAY BANDOLIER

Bandoliers (ban-duh-LEERZ), or shoulder bags, were made by women and worn by men. They took over a year to make.

Hollow bugle beads came from traders.

Dentalia shells looked like teeth.

Beads, shells, and elk teeth decorated clothing.

Elk tooth

Cowrie shells

MITTENS

Mittens were made of animal skin and wool from traders. The fur on the inside kept fingers warm and toasty.

FROM BONE TO STEEL

Indian women sewed with bone needles and sinew thread made from buffalo tendons, until white traders brought steel needles and cotton thread.

BASIN·DASIN

Women wove beautiful beaded sashes and bags on looms.

Little Sweden

The Larsons liked to talk about Sweden and to remember all they had left behind. Their memories pulled at their heartstrings every day and made them feel split between the old land and the new. This "divided heart" caused Swedish immigrants to form close-knit communities and to hold on to many of their Swedish traditions. At the same time, however, children like Kirsten needed to learn both the language and the customs of their new home. It was up to them to plant deep roots in America.

SWEDISH KEEPSAKES
Precious linens, sashes, and clothes made by loved ones in Sweden were kept safe in hand-painted boxes.

"Maypole" is an American way of saying the Swedish word "majstang" (MY-stang). **Maja** *means "to decorate with greenery" and* **stang** *means "pole."*

MIDSUMMER
Midsummer is a Scandinavian celebration of light and warmth. It's held in June on the longest day of the year. On this day in Sweden, the sun never sets. People dance and feast all night long!

SWEDISH CHRISTMAS
In Sweden, Christmas was celebrated for a whole month. Pioneers in America couldn't take that much time, but they still celebrated just as they had in Sweden.

① *Candles were precious, but on Christmas Eve Swedish families sometimes lit one in each window to show the way for Jultomten.*

Families left rice pudding out for Jultomten, the Swedish Christmas elf.

WOVEN CLOTHS
Swedes stored their handwoven cloths and clothing by draping them over their ceiling beams.

CHURCH
The Swedish-American church was important to immigrants. It was a place of worship, but also where Swedish Americans gathered for picnics, socials, and meetings.

Pattern and pins

Drum

Bobbins and thread

BOBBIN LACE
Swedish women made bobbin lace by wrapping a paper pattern around a drum. They placed pins in the pattern holes and wound threads around the pins to weave beautiful, delicate designs.

② *Colorful toy horses with traditional painted designs are a handicraft from Dalarna, Sweden.*

③ *Children made decorations from straw in their families' barns.*

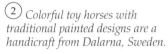

A psalmodiken (sohl-MO-dih-ken) is a traditional Swedish one-stringed instrument. It accompanied the singing at church on Sunday.

Hymnal

Minnesota's Settlers

The Minnesota frontier was dotted with close-knit farming settlements of Swedes, Germans, and Norwegians. Yankees from the New England states came to the frontier, too. They built new towns, taught in one-room schools, and started small businesses. In Kirsten's time, Minnesota was a mixture of New England, New Sweden, New Norway, and New Germany—right in the middle of America.

YANKEES
Minnesota's first teacher was a Yankee named Harriet Bishop. She came west because she felt she was needed in St. Paul "more than in any other spot on earth."

Yankees built homes like those they had left back East. Many had crisp, white clapboard siding and orderly picket fences.

GERMANS
Kirsten had lots of German neighbors. In Germany, young children went to preschools called *kindergartens*, German for "child garden." When Margarethe Schurz came to America from Germany in the 1850s, she started the first kindergarten in America.

Germans decorated plates and furniture with brightly colored floral and geometric patterns.

Norwegian cloth

Rosemaling was done by Norwegians as well as Swedes. Norway and Sweden share many traditions because the countries are right next to each other.

NORWEGIANS

The church was the center of Norwegian-American communities. They formed youth groups, choirs, and ladies' aid societies. They held picnics and served traditional Norwegian foods such as *lutefisk* (LOOT-fisk), or fish soaked in lye, and a flat bread called *lefse* (LEF-suh).

Wood was scarce in Germany, so homes were made mostly with brick or mud. In America, Germans built their homes the same way.

Germans grew grapes and berries that made wonderful wines and preserves.

German wood carving

A Trip to Town

Every time a family like the Larsons came to town, there was something new to see. There might be a new church, a school, a bank, a drugstore, or a hotel—maybe even with a big, shiny dance floor! As small towns grew into bustling communities, there were more reasons to come back as often as possible.

One reason pioneer families came to town was to celebrate the Fourth of July. Everyone, no matter what country they were from, looked forward to the holiday. They loaded the summer's produce into their wagons and headed to town to trade and celebrate America's birthday.

THE GENERAL STORE
The general store was one of the first businesses in a frontier town. Settlers, trappers, and Indians came to trade. Pioneer families picked up mail, bought supplies, and heard news of the outside world.

Settlers might have traded honeycomb for tools or other goods they couldn't make themselves.

From the book *Kirsten's Surprise*

THE FOURTH OF JULY
Kirsten first celebrated the Fourth of July in 1855. Families of many nationalities gathered to honor America's birthday. Hardworking adults and children were treated to parades, races, games, picnics, and thrilling fireworks.

Settlers had to pay postage when they received letters, but not when they mailed them!

*Anders Larson
Maryville
Minnesota Territory*

IN A PIG'S EYE!

St. Paul, the bustling capital of Minnesota, started as a small group of rowdy settlers. The most well-known was "Pig's Eye"—a man with one good eye and one very ugly blind eye. He was so memorable, the settlement became known as Pig's Eye. In 1841, a bishop came to "clean up" Pig's Eye. One of the first things he did was rename the settlement St. Paul.

GROWING TOWNS

As a town grew, dressmakers, druggists, and grocers opened shops separate from the general store. When a town was big enough, it would open its own United States Post Office. New businesses, like sawmills or newspaper offices, would soon follow.

For a girl like Kirsten, there were pretty ribbons to gaze at and, if she was lucky, hard candies to taste at the general store.

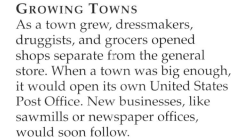

INDIANS IN TOWN

If white settlers visited the small towns near the Dakota reservation lands, they would see Indians buying and trading goods. A few Indians worked for white families in these towns. Others came to trade fur or quillwork for warm blankets.

45

The Reservation

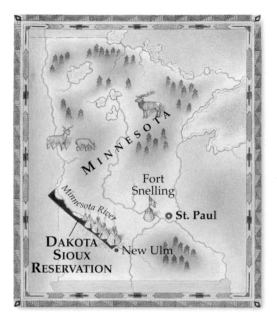

By 1858, all of Singing Bird's people were crowded onto a thin strip of land along the Minnesota River. The money the U.S. government owed them had come in droplets. Often it hadn't come at all. Some Dakota became so angry they threatened white people.

The Dakota had also begun to argue among themselves. They were split between those who tried to live in the traditional way, by hunting and gathering, and those who tried to live like white people, by farming. White missionaries and government officials also urged the Dakota to give up their traditional clothing, homes, and even their language—everything that made them Dakota.

Hunting was hard because there were few animals on the reservation.

GOVERNMENT SUPPLIES
Between government payments, Indians had to buy food on credit so they would not starve. This drawing shows an Indian agent handing out supplies. If he didn't receive payment, he might ask for double the next time.

Indian women were given cloth, needles, and thread so they could sew clothes for themselves and their families.

CUT-HAIRS
Cut-hairs were Indian men who wore white men's hairstyles and clothes. The government gave these Indians plots of land and built them brick houses. But most Dakota did not want to give up their way of life.

RESERVATION SCHOOLS
Missionaries set up schools like the one shown below. The children had to give up their Indian culture—even their own names—to learn white ways. One student remembered, "They took away our language so that we would lose our spirit."

"THEN EAT GRASS!"

In the summer of 1861, Minnesota's crops failed. The Dakota survived the winter on what little corn and potatoes they were able to grow. By June of 1862, they desperately needed the money the U.S. government owed them. It didn't arrive.

The Dakota knew that part of the reason for the late payment was the government's attention to another matter— the Civil War. The whole country was at war, North against South.

Posters encouraged Minnesota men to fight in the Civil War.

Weeks went by, and finally a group of young Dakota men approached a white trader named Andrew Myrick. They told him if they didn't receive the money they were owed, they would starve. Myrick laughed at them and said, "Then eat grass!"

Anger burned inside the Dakota men. They knew that the strongest white men were far away, fighting in the Civil War. They thought the time was right to reclaim their lost lands.

Eggs Start War

It all started as a dare. On August 17, 1862, four young Dakota men found some hen's eggs at a white settler's farm. They dared one man to steal them. When the settlers came outside, the Dakota men killed them. Then the men ran to a nearby Dakota village and begged their people to protect them and to join in their fight. The next day, the Dakota attacked the government agency on the reservation. They raided the warehouse, took supplies, and killed anyone who tried to stop them. The Dakota Conflict had begun.

LITTLE CROW
The Dakota leader Little Crow knew the Dakota would never win the war. "You are fools," he told them. "But I am not a coward. I will die with you."

During a battle, Little Crow wore an eagle-feathered war-bonnet to show his power.

Sarah Wakefield and Chaska

Sarah and John Wakefield were well respected by the Dakota Indians. As the reservation doctor, John Wakefield had treated many of the Dakota. His wife Sarah had often joined the Dakota women as they cooked and sewed.

When news of the Dakota's attack spread, John arranged for Sarah and their two young children to be taken to the safety of nearby Fort Ridgely. While they were on the road, they were attacked by two Dakota warriors. One of the Dakota, a man named Chaska, recognized Sarah as a friend. He told his fellow warrior not to kill the white woman and her children. Chaska took them to a Dakota village.

When the conflict was over, Chaska was sentenced to die for his participation. Sarah Wakefield spoke out and said that she and her children would not be alive were it not for Chaska. Many people criticized Sarah for defending Chaska. Her pleas did not save him.

FORT SNELLING
The news of the conflict sent panic throughout the towns of Minnesota. Farmers and towns-people within a hundred miles headed for the safety of Fort Snelling, where soldiers were training for the Civil War.

HELD CAPTIVE
Many settlers were held captive in Dakota villages. Some were killed. Others were spared because they were friends of the Dakota.

LED TO SAFETY
Not all the Dakota joined in the conflict. Some, like John Other Day, led settlers like those at left to safe places such as St. Paul.

A Captive's Story

When the Dakota Conflict began, 14-year-old Mary Schmidt was boarding with a family several miles from her own family's farm. On the morning of August 18, 1862, Mary was busy working, when suddenly someone shouted that the Indians were coming and everyone should head into the open prairie. Mary and several others climbed into the back of a wagon and hurried away, headed for safety. A short while later, they were captured by the Dakota.

Mary was taken to Little Crow's village and placed in a tepee with other white captives. After a while a young Dakota woman came in and spoke to Mary in English. "I have bought you from that bad Indian who captured you," she explained. "He was going to kill you, so I have given him my pony. . . . Now you are going to be my daughter."

The woman's name was Snana, and she gave Mary a buckskin dress, brightly decorated with beads. She also gave Mary beads for her neck, a pair of moccasins, and a white blanket. Then Snana took Mary's hair down and made two braids. Where her part was, Snana painted Mary's scalp red. Finally, Snana dabbed a red dot under each of Mary's eyes. "You must now call me Mother," Snana said.

Snana was a kind mother and protected Mary during her captivity. Once Little Crow gave an order to kill all the whites in the camp. Snana dug a hole, made Mary get into it, and then covered it with buffalo skin to hide her. Another time, as Mary sat outside the tepee door holding Snana's youngest child, Little Crow passed by. Suddenly, he stopped and raised his tomahawk over Mary's head as though he would kill her. She sat perfectly still, and he finally lowered it and walked away.

Mary lived as Snana's daughter for two months, until she was released by U.S. Army soldiers. Despite the terror of her captivity, Mary never forgot the Dakota woman's kindness and protection. The two visited each other and exchanged letters— Snana addressing the letters "My dear daughter"— until Snana died in 1908.

My dear daughter, ... I think about you as my own child... I feel like I went to your house and saw you while I was writing to you.

— your mother, Snana

Mary and Snana pose
for a photographer
in the 1890s.

The Battles of New Ulm

The German settlement of New Ulm was the largest town near the Dakota reservation. It was attacked twice. While the men of New Ulm organized an army, women and children crowded into buildings along the main street. The town hotel became so crowded that, as a young boy remembered, the women had to go outside and take off their hoopskirts so they wouldn't keep bumping into one another. "We laughed in spite of our danger," he recalled.

Only a few of the white settlers owned rifles. They also defended themselves with clubs and pitchforks.

TWO ATTACKS
At the first attack on New Ulm, the settlers were able to hold off the Dakota warriors until a thunderstorm ended the fighting. Five days later, the Dakota returned. The attack lasted all day, and many of the buildings in New Ulm were burned.

ONE VICTORY

The men, women, and children of New Ulm finally succeeded in driving off the Dakota. The settlers had won that battle, but other Minnesota towns still desperately needed help.

CALLING THE TROOPS

Minnesota needed the help of the soldiers who were fighting in the Civil War. Minnesota's governor asked President Lincoln for his troops back. The soldiers returned to defend their own state against the Dakota.

Helen Tarble and Her Neighbors

The Dakota and the German residents of New Ulm had never gotten along well. Back in the fall of 1854, the Germans staked their claim for the town site. That winter, they took over nearby Dakota hunting grounds as well. The Dakota fought back, but the residents of New Ulm wouldn't give up. The land was not officially theirs, but with the help of a U.S. senator, they were allowed to keep it.

Helen Tarble lived in Beaver Creek, near New Ulm, and often visited the Dakota villages across the river. When the conflict began, Helen and her family were with settlers fleeing New Ulm. When the Dakota attacked them, Helen spoke to them in their language, pleading for the lives of her family. Because Helen was their friend, she and her family survived the attack and were led to safety.

Language books and Bibles may have helped Helen learn the Dakota language.

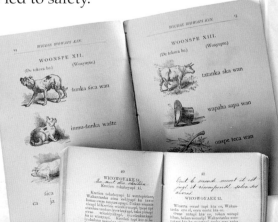

Aftermath

After six weeks of fighting, the Minnesota soldiers and settlers forced the Dakota to surrender. Many Dakota warriors fled further west, or north into Canada. The rest of the Dakota, including men, women, and children who had not fought at all, were taken to Fort Snelling for trial. More than three hundred Dakota were sentenced to die. But at President Lincoln's request, most of the sentences were changed to prison terms. Still, on December 26, 1862, thirty-eight Dakota died by hanging.

TAKEN PRISONER
One Dakota girl named Good Star Woman told about being taken to Fort Snelling. Settlers carrying poles and pitchforks jeered and poked at them. Soldiers rode alongside the Dakota to protect them, but many Dakota were hurt.

FORT SNELLING
The Dakota who were taken to Fort Snelling camped on the land where they had danced and played games in happier times. They stayed in the prison camp through the entire winter. Many died from illness or starvation.

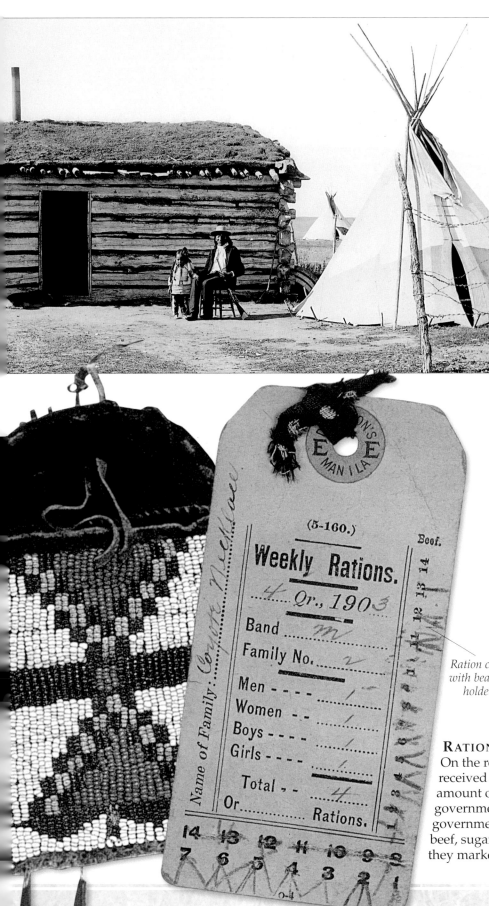

PUSHED OUT

After the war, the Dakota were pushed out of Minnesota and onto reservations farther west. Once again, white people wanted them to give up their "Indian ways." But that did not happen entirely. They built log houses like the settlers but built tepees right beside them.

Doll and carrier made in 1993

Ration card with beaded holder

RATION CARDS

On the reservation, the Dakota received *rations*, or a limited amount of supplies, from the government. Each time the government agents handed out beef, sugar, flour, or other supplies, they marked the ration cards.

(5-160.) Beef.

Weekly Rations.

4 Qr., 1903

Band ____ M

Family No. ____ 2

Men ____ 1

Women ____ 1

Boys ____ 1

Girls ____ 1

Total ____ 4

Or. ____ Rations.

Name of Family: Coulee Nichlaw

The Dakota Today

Today, many Dakota Indians still live on reservations and in cities across the United States. They are proud of their past and carry on many Dakota customs. Some Indian women still teach their daughters to quill and bead in the hope of keeping these traditional arts alive.

Many Dakota also hold ceremonies or gatherings called *powwows*. At a powwow, the Dakota often join with other Indian tribes to dance, sing, and share food and drink. The children hear stories and songs in their native language and listen to their elders repeat the legends they learned from their own parents and grandparents.

The Dakota, as well as other Indian tribes, have struggled to hold on to their traditions and to pass them on to younger generations. One Dakota woman said, "We were oppressed, but we can say that we have survived."

Traditional beadwork on modern tennis shoes

Into the Wild West

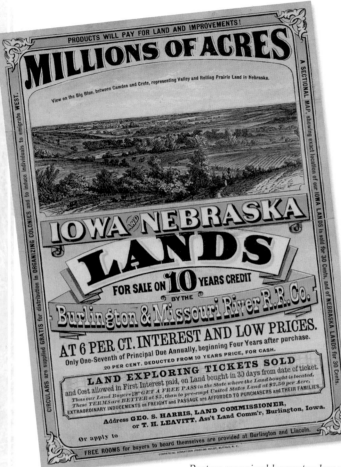

After the Dakota Conflict, settlers were eager to farm the lands the Indians had lost. Both the president and the growing railroad companies believed the sooner the West was settled, the sooner America would be rich and powerful.

In 1862, President Lincoln signed the Homestead Act into law. Anyone over 21 could pay a small fee to claim up to 160 acres of western land. If settlers built homes and farmed the land, it was theirs free and clear. One homesteader recalled that "every imagination was fired with dreams and visions of new homes and fortunes to be made in the fertile West."

Posters promised homesteaders rich farmland along the railroad routes.

MAKING TRACKS
In 1869, the first *transcontinental*, or cross-country, railroad was completed. Towns sprang up along its tracks all across America. White settlers felt that the railroad brought safety and civilization to the western wilderness.

LAND RUSH!
In the Oklahoma Territory, homesteaders rushed the land. They lined the boundaries of the territory and waited for a starting signal. Then people raced in on horseback, in trains and wagons, and on foot to stake a claim.

NATURAL WONDERS
Paintings and photographs made the West seem like a paradise on earth. People were amazed by the breathtaking mountains, hot springs, geysers, and waterfalls.

BEAUTY IN A HARSH LAND
Most homesteaders had no idea how difficult their lives would be. They found tough earth, dust storms, and blizzards. Those who stayed turned the prairie into America's most productive farm-land. One woman wrote, *"When we got in our first crop of wheat I used to . . . watch it wave as the wind blew over it and think I had never seen anything so beautiful."*

A Peek into the Future

At last America was beginning to feel like home—with good food, a real bed to sleep in, and best of all, friends.

—Meet Kirsten

When Kirsten crossed the Atlantic Ocean to come to America, she was nine years old. By the end of the Dakota Conflict, she would have been a young woman of 17. What was her life like during those years? She might have seen loved ones go off to fight in the Civil War. She and Singing Bird had to say good-bye, but they might have written letters to each other all their lives, just as Mary and Snana did.

Kirsten surely spent lots of time with Anna and Lisbeth in their secret fort, daydreaming about being grown up. She might have braided strands of her golden hair into jewelry or tried to walk in a poufy hoopskirt. And of course she went to barn dances and started sparking. She may even have had to refuse a man with too many mangles!

By the time Kirsten turned 17, she probably would have been married. She and her husband might have decided to homestead in the Wild West. They might have packed up all their precious belongings and headed west for places like the Nebraska Territory, Oregon, or California—names that sounded as strange to Kirsten as Minnesota once had.

Kirsten would have been very sad to leave her home and family for the second time in her life. As one woman homesteader remembered, *"To say I wept bitterly would but faintly express the ocean of tears I shed on leaving my beloved home."* When Mama said good-bye, she could comfort Kirsten with the same words Mormor used when the Larsons left Sweden: "When you're lonely, look at the sun. Remember that we all see the same sun."